LOW'S CARTOON HISTORY
1945-1953

LOW'S CARTOON HISTORY

1945-1953

By

DAVID LOW

NEW YORK

SIMON & SCHUSTER

1953

PRINTED IN GREAT BRITAIN
COLLINS CLEAR-TYPE PRESS: LONDON AND GLASGOW

FOREWORD

A POLITICAL cartoonist for a daily newspaper is circumscribed by two conditions, timeliness and topicality. The clock ticks and he must tick with it. Indeed, allowing for the delays of the processes whereby his works reach the public, well ahead of it. So much so, that he must of necessity cultivate foresight, learn to measure events and anticipate their consequences in time to meet them punctually when they happen.

An optimistic philosopher once said that a clear-minded troglodyte who was present at, say, the invention of the wheel, ought to have been able from that point onward to deduce the course of Man: the development of industry, trade rivalries, national wars, power groups, world wars, the readjustment violent and otherwise of social systems, world government, the conquest of space, of time, of life itself, and so on. Making allowance for science, aesthetics, ethics and religion, all this he could have foreseen in smooth logical progression of cause and effect. Or should have, were it not for one important factor—Man himself. Because of the eccentricity of human behaviour, Man is unpredictable, not to be counted on to do the wise thing. Nor even, for the matter of that, to make a fool of himself.

The inevitable is unavoidable, of course. But the road to it is frequently not so much smooth and logical as bumpy and whimsical. No doubt it would be more convenient for political cartoonists if everything happened as it should happen, at the right time, in the right place, in the right way. Certainly the daily effort first to abstract the gist of separate political slips, shocks and staggers as they happen; then to correlate these to the larger global disturbances; and finally to comment satirically upon their significance before they have passed from " topicality " altogether, makes what would otherwise be a pleasant profession into an exacting one.

One may be so wise long after the event as to claim that it was predictable a decade beforehand, that, say, in 1917 the Czar would be ass enough to present Russia on a plate to his revolutionaries; or that there would be a Hitler; and that he would gamble on World War II, although it was certain in advance that he could never get away with it. But who, in 1945, could have foreseen that the realists of Moscow would turn into mystics and pass up the chance of a 25-year alliance with U.S.A. (with all the political and economic dividends that could have been made to pay) to follow a chancy policy which automatically brought into being a gigantic array of force against them? And, that, having done so, they would reverse engines to back up to starting point? Who, again, could have expected that American Capitalism would find the wisdom to extend its life by acting on the maxim It is Better To Give Than To Receive? Who expected that the lesson of the agony endured by the Jews under the Nazis would be the efficacy of propaganda plus ruthless force?

Such irrational derangements as these are disconcerting. International politics become a Mystery Ride instead of an orderly tour, mapped and charted. Prophets begin to doubt their own powers of calculation and intuition. Their revised chains of probabilities carry larger question marks. Can one remain reasonably confident that the British Commonwealth will fuse with the United States of America? Is it certain that Germany will dominate Europe? Will Communism surely split in twain, its centrifugal point moving to Pekin, leaving the Political Church of Lenin to the leadership of Tito, backed by Wall Street? Can one be positive that Science will produce a corrective for the hydrogen bomb? Will the full application of atomic energy to industry inevitably make Private Enterprise impossible, finally dispose of the wages system altogether and present Man with a Golden Age? . . . Perhaps not, after all. These maybe but speculations of the imagination to be accepted with reserve.

In assembling this collection of cartoons after sufficient lapse of time for their significance to become apparent, there is a temptation to doctor and revise individual items so that they might seem wiser, wittier and more prescient than they were at the time. But honesty has prevailed, and the drawings appear here as when they were first published in the *Evening Standard*, the *Daily Herald* or the *Manchester Guardian*, except that labels and names included as necessary for identification in newspaper publication have been removed as redundant now all are collected in a book; that the drawings have been " reframed " in a new border-line to suit the page-size of the book; that titles have been changed in two or three cases for greater clarity; and that occasional departures from date sequence have been made to bring together cartoons on the same subject.

These liberties taken, one might expect the pictures to be left to tell their own story. But symbolism and analogy are highly subjective, and a cartoon that wanders beyond moronic simplicity seems therefore to be capable of an infinite number of interpretations. A short statement under each cartoon of the matters that inspired it shows that in this case the artist decided to get in first.

London, June 1953   DAVID LOW

LOW'S CARTOON HISTORY
1945-1953

INTRODUCTION

UNDER THE INFLUENCE

4 November 1940

When Hitler bargained with Molotov in 1940 he made a last try to talk Russia out of South-Eastern Europe. But Molotov stood out for his two stock ideas: security arrangements with Bulgaria and Turkey; and a Soviet base in the Dardanelles. The more Hitler argued, the more Molotov stiffened his attitude.

"I SAID 'PLEASE SPEAK MORE DISTINCTLY'"

28 October 1943

Salvoes for Russian victories were booming when Foreign Ministers Hull (U S) and Eden (Britain) visited Moscow in 1943. They wanted to talk about the future of the small States bordering on Russia, but Molotov was deaf in that ear. The Soviet Government had already determined to make its own post-war security system without outside interference.

LOOKING TOWARDS WASHINGTON

20 February 1945

The end of the war found the world " magnificently unprepared " for peace. Europe looked to the U S as the one belligerent with its riches and industrial mechanism intact and even greatly extended, hoping for not only the means but the inspiration to reconstruction.

"BABY PLAY WITH NICE BALL?"

9 August 1945

The release of atomic energy brought a question to the human race: would Man, so ingenious in invention, apply the new discovery to the constructive arts of peace, creating for himself immeasurable material betterment ? Or would he, so immature in reflection, use it as yet another means to the conquest of power. thereby risking his own utter destruction?

SAME OLD GAME

YOUR MOVE NEXT, BYRNES

20 September 1945

The tension of war relaxed, the victors began to think of peace in terms of their own security. When the Foreign Ministers met, Secretary Byrnes, for the United States, was unwilling to quit the American bases in the Pacific without first being assured of full military and strategic rights at points " necessary for complete protection of U S interest and world peace." On the other hand, Foreign Minister Molotov, for the USSR, was out to protect the Russian frontier by forming a chain of buffer states across Europe, with a strategic anchor in the Mediterranean.

BEHIND THE CURTAIN

25 September 1945

It became evident that Moscow, pursuing the buffer-chain idea, was deliberately establishing complete political and economic domination over the former Axis satellite countries in Eastern Europe. Byrnes and Bevin protested that to help Communist minorities to " fix " voting conditions so as to return stooge governments was not the way to hold the " free elections " agreed at Yalta. Molotov denied using pressure, insisted that the governments enjoyed majority support and invited the Foreign Ministers to mind their own business. Byrnes and Bevin were not satisfied.

ARGUMENT ON A WALL

18 December 1945

When Lend-Lease was suddenly cut off in 1945, Britain desperately needed hard cash to avoid cuts in food, materials and capital goods. Lord Keynes was sent to America to raise a loan. Finally Washington drove a hard bargain with Lord Halifax. Whereby Britain promised to sign the Bretton Woods agreement and to place her financial policies under the supervisions of the International Monetary Fund; and to underwrite American world trade plans, including the " multi-lateral free market " and contraction of Britain's Imperial preferences. The British feared that the terms might hinder the realisation of their full-employment policy and a planned Socialist economy.

12

HAUNTED QUEUE

19 September 1945

After the wastage and neglect of the war the food position,
especially in the Far East, was very bad. It seemed that
famine could be avoided only if available resources of the
world were organised and distributed month by month,
territory by territory; and if, while the world's supplies
were short, the people that had enough were willing to
deprive themselves for the benefit of those who had not.

UNITED SURGERY IN EUROPE

26 October 1945

Under the Potsdam agreement dismembered Germany was to be de-militarised and de-industrialised to prevent a war of revenge, and then administered as one economic whole. But its main food area was already incorporated in Poland together with the Silesian industrial belt; and if its heavy industry in the West were to be dismantled, firstly, the Germans would have no means of support, and secondly, Europe would be deprived of production necessary for recovery. The French held that the safest course would be to postpone centralising the administration and to incorporate the Ruhr and Rhineland industries into Western Europe. Moscow complained this was an anti-Russian idea because it would vastly cut reparations. Washington disliked it for different reasons. But the problem remained.

14

WHY CAN'T WE WORK TOGETHER IN MUTUAL TRUST AND CONFIDENCE?

30 October 1945

President Truman made a speech on twelve principles underlying U S foreign policy, which included refusal to recognise any government imposed on any nation by a foreign Power; and the outlawing of the atomic bomb by world co-operation. Until international control justified its atomic secrets being shared with others, the U S would hold them as a sacred trust. Moscow retorted nastily that since the secrets were not to be revealed forthwith, it was evident that some Americans wished their country to keep and use the bomb as an instrument of national policy.

15

DIFFICULT COURTSHIP

2 November 1945

After Truman's speech, the conference of Foreign Ministers broke down and the temperature fell to freezing. Moscow said that Truman's interference in Russia's arrangements for Bulgaria, Rumania and Hungary arose from a wish to weaken Soviet security, and that his refusal to turn the atom bomb over to the United Nations at once showed his warmongering intentions. During a spell of cold uneasiness, Byrnes and Bevin offered Molotov a twenty-five-year treaty of alliance as an alternative to his own ideas of security, and an invitation to play a leading part in international control of the bomb. But in vain.

PHEW, IT'S TIME SOMEONE PROVIDED AN UNRRA FOR UNRRAS

16 January 1946

UNRRA, the international organisation for helping to sustain and rehabilitate war damaged countries until they could look after themselves, was under heavy strain, partly because its work and development had been far greater than had been expected, and partly because commensurate support had not been forthcoming from the fifty-one member-nations of UNO.

"JUST TO POUR ON THE TROUBLED WATERS"

29 January 1946

A " democratic movement " arose in northern Iran, when
rebels, helped by Soviet troops left behind after the world
war, sought to set up Azabaijan as an autonymous state.
Despite Russian objections, the matter came before the
Security Council at UNO. After stormy exchanges, Russia
consented to move out (and forgo the possibilities of setting
up a new satellite state to worry Turkey) if the Iranian
Government met their rather stiff demands for oil concessions in the North. Bevin and Vishinsky, the new Soviet
Foreign Minister, each considering Iranian oil vital to his
national defence, assured one another that his wish was only
to preserve order.

COME DOWN TO EARTH

15 February 1946

Failure of the monsoon had driven the food situation from
bad to worse for the 500 million people in India and the
East. Five to fifteen million Indians were threatened with
death from starvation, and conditions in Malaya were
nearly as bad. The United Nations were made aware by
urgent messages from the Director-General of UNRRA
that food came before politics as the first and greatest
problem of the Far East.

RUSSIAN BALLET——SLEEPLESS BEAUTY

21 February 1946

A hue and cry arose in Canada after the news that counter-espionage authorities had discovered a large Russian spy-service and that twelve persons had been arrested near Ottawa charged with disclosure of official secrets to a foreign Power. Washington was greatly disturbed lest some of the atom secrets in Canada's possession had "leaked." The Soviet Government admitted that "individual collaborators" had obtained "unimportant technical data," but accused the Canadian Government of making a fuss about nothing, to damage the Soviet Union.

PICKET LINE

6 March 1946

An Anglo-French-American statement on Spain, issued
with captured German documents, revealed that in June
1940 Franco promised both Hitler and Mussolini to join
their side in the war on condition that Spain received
Gibraltar, French Morocco and part of Algeria. The U S
asked France and Britain to join in offering help to any
new government in Spain that would displace Franco's
régime, which was described in France as a danger to
peace. Franco calculated that his critics, Bidault, Bevin
and Byrnes, already had their hands full and without
interrupting a new list of political executions made a
rude noise.

AT ARM'S LENGTH

7 March 1946

The Soviet spy-hunt in Canada and the Anglo-American interference with Russian moves in Iran and south-east Europe, particularly in Bulgaria, did not sweeten Moscow's temper towards Britain or the U S. The Moscow press played down a conciliatory speech from Bevin offering to extend Britain's treaty of alliance with Russia, made before the UN existed, to fifty years, and began a campaign of bitter abuse, accusing Britain of bolstering up dying reactionary régimes such as Persia and Greece. Friendliness did not suit Russia's book.

INQUEST ON THE CHURCHILL ATOM-BOMB EXPERIMENT

8 March 1946

" Nobody knows what Russia intends to do, or what are the limits, if any, of its expansion," said Winston Churchill, in a speech at Fulton, Missouri. He called for an intimate relationship, air, military and naval, between the British Commonwealth and the United States. Although Churchill had no official position, Soviet spokesmen greeted this as a spectacular break of British policy, pointing out that a military alliance of two of the three Great Powers against the other meant the end of the Big Three Coalition.

23

"WHAT ARE YOU LOOKING FOR, JOE? MAYBE WE CAN HELP YOU FIND IT"

3 April 1946

Russia's negative attitude and her uncompromising rebuffs to friendly approaches reduced Bevin at last to something like bewildered exasperation. Britain and the U S wished to settle the question of Middle East oil by agreement, but the Russian delegate walked out of the Security Council. "Will the Soviet Government say what it wants?" asked Bevin. "Cannot disputes between the Great Powers about vital raw materials be settled without reverting to the old imperialism, power politics and force?"

"NOW THAT WINSTON AND ERNIE HAVE ESTABLISHED DEMOCRACY ON A FIRM BASIS I'LL SOON BE GOING HOME, I DON'T SUPPOSE"

"PEACE" IN GREECE

11 April 1946

There was some justification for the Soviet's charges against Britain concerning Greece. The British supported a shaky Greek Coalition Government with troops, money and goods against the threat of Communist-Republican revolution. Bevin decided that the first step to stabilisation was to hold immediate elections. Left-wing parties complained that the electoral registers were obsolete or faked, and boycotted the voting. Seven Ministers resigned, protesting that Britain was turning the country over to the Fascists. Even the Premier admitted the elections would be unfair and that only monarchist candidates could move freely. The elections were held. The monarchists won.

NOW ALL YOU HAVE TO DO IS TO GET ASHORE

2 May 1946

The Report of the Anglo-American Palestine Committee recommended that 100,000 immigrants be admitted during 1946. Palestine should be neither a Jewish or an Arab State. Government should continue under British mandate until the UN could arrange a trusteeship. Britain, the mandatory called on to implement the recommendations, added that first the Jews and the Arabs should disarm. But the Arab League opposed the Report absolutely; the Jews wanted the 100,000 immigrants without disarming, and the Jewish Agency dissembled when asked to help in suppressing the illegal armies. Assassination, terrorism and sabotage continued.

HEADS IN THE SAND

10 May 1946

When Britain opened negotiations with Egypt to consolidate their alliance as between two equal nations, and
promised to evacuate all British forces from Egypt the
Attlee Government was criticised as " giving away the
Empire " by those who did not realise that the world had
changed and plans for the defence of the Commonwealth
must change with it. In days of jet-planes and atom-bombs,
alliances and mutual assistance pacts offered better prospect
for the security of the Commonwealth " life-line " through
the Suez Canal than a series of new wars to destroy the
growth of nationalism in the Middle East.

FROM LAND TO MOUTH

26 August 1946

Boyd Orr at the newly formed Food and Agricultural
Organisation called for a World Food Board to stabilise
international market prices and to build up a world
reserve of food to level out good and bad harvests. At
first the U S, as well as other big food-growing countries,
approved, and Russia and Argentina were asked to join.
But while they doubted, the U S Government was influenced
by American farming interests to reverse its policy, and
threw the idea down. Then the question was how to get
America's rich harvest to customers who could not pay
for it.

"IF WE DON'T LET HIM WORK, WHO'S GOING TO KEEP HIM?"

12 July 1946

The unsolved problem of Germany's future continued to vex the Foreign Ministers. According to Molotov, it was understood at Yalta that Russia was entitled to 10,000 million dollars worth of reparations from Germany in equipment and current production. Byrnes replied that that figure had been only a basis for discussion. Anyway, Yalta had been superseded by Potsdam where it had been agreed that Germany should be left with sufficient resources to permit her to exist without outside help. Germany as an economic whole could not exist if the surplus production of one zone were taken as reparations without reference to the needs of other zones.

LIFE, LIBERTY AND THE PURSUIT OF HAPPINESS

23 July 1946

Conditions in the United States were inflationary and the cost of living was rising, accompanied and accentuated by labour troubles. Higher wages conceded without reference to fixed prices weakened the foundations of the wages-prices control, and Congress drafted a new Bill in effect bringing price control to an end. Some observers feared that it might become impossible to keep the cost of living in any reasonable ratio to wages and income. The unions got ready with wage demands.

DOWN BARRIERS IN GERMANY

1 August 1946

The lop-sided consequences of operating half a treaty were demonstrated when Soviet Russia insisted on taking reparations from current production in the Eastern zone instead of making its surplus resources available to the West. To feed and keep Western Germany going in 1946 had cost the U S 200 million dollars and Britain 80 million pounds. For economy and efficiency the two democracies merged the administration of their zones. Moscow professed to see this as a sinister move to make the division of Germany permanent.

SEARCH FOR AN OPEN DOOR

2 August 1946

A million and a half displaced persons still remained in
Europe. It was evident that new homes must be found
overseas for large numbers, and member Governments of
the United Nations were asked each to receive a proportion,
including Jews. Britain had already accepted and promised
to promote re-settlement of about 300,000, the U S
275,000, and more were to go to South American
countries. But plans elsewhere lagged. The question of
the limits of Palestine's capacity to receive new immigrants
without political and economic upheaval was being argued
with guns.

"SORRY, DUCKS, THIS ONE'S TAKEN"

DARDANELLES
DEFENCE BLOCKHOUSE

FEAR
OF
RUSSIA

RUSSIA'S
FEAR

LOW

MEDITERRANEAN SQUATTERS

21 August 1946

Soviet Russia proposed to Turkey that the Montreux Convention be revised to make the organisation of the defence of the Dardanelles the joint concern of Turkey and the USSR, as the Powers most interested and capable. But America objected that the régime of the Straits was a concern also of other Powers, including the U S, and, if the Straits became the object of aggression, of the United Nations. Russia's proposal, which might have been seen in a friendly light earlier, was now regarded with suspicion.

VERDICT

1 October 1946

The International Tribunal at Nuremberg delivered judgment on the Nazi war criminals and organisations. The Nazi leadership was found guilty beyond the shadow of a doubt, and Goering, Ribbentrop, Keitel, Kaltenbrunner, Rosenberg, Frick, Frank, Streicher, Sauckel, Jodl, Seyss-Inquart and Bormann were sentenced to be hanged. Apart from UNRRA, the trial was the sole instance of international co-operation since the end of the war.

WELL, THAT'S THE END OF THE NAZIS

4 October 1946

Between American Free Enterprise and Russian Communism the German people had had a confusing year. The Russians exploited their zone but the German population was fully employed and under a rationing system benefiting those who worked hard. In the Anglo-American bi-zone there was large-scale unemployment. The victors having no plans, they provided the Germans with no targets and no incentives. Incompetence, inefficiency and uncertainty inspired no confidence in the future of democracy in Germany.

NEED FOR SOME REARRANGEMENT

15 October 1946

Britain and the U S were prepared to fulfil the conditions laid down by the Potsdam Agreement provided it applied to all four zones so that Germany as a whole would be self-supporting. But for Byrnes and Bevin, getting West Germany going without its natural source of supply in East Germany was like trying to run a truck without its front wheels. Molotov, who had already incorporated those front wheels in a Russian machine, put the difficulties of his colleagues down to sheer inefficiency and incompetence.

MILLSTONE

24 October 1946

When Britain and the U S complained about the situation
in Germany Russia always replied, " Look up your Potsdam." Russia's operation of Potsdam meant for Britain
and the U S their being burdened with the heavy costs of
buying food and other goods to send to West Germany
while the Russians were taking similar stocks from East
Germany to Russia. In addition they had to contend with
the disturbance among German Social Democrats who did
not relish committing political suicide by conniving at the
rebuilding of the German trusts, with or without Anglo-
American control.

37

TOO MUCH EMPHASIS ON THE "NO"

25 October 1946

Russia's frequent use of the veto to obstruct business in the Security Council had become a wry joke. When the UN Charter was framed the veto was understood as being applicable only concerning sanctions, but Russia had used it in such a way as to prevent the investigation of facts and to obstruct pacific settlement of disputes. Exasperated small powers in the UN Assembly asked for a restriction of its use. Molotov claimed that the power of veto was basic and if it were weakened the United Nations would end. After that, UNO, represented here by Assembly President Evatt and Secretary-General Trygve Lie, decided not to tinker with the principle of unanimity.

"WOULD YOU MIND TURNING OFF THE RADIO? CAN'T HEAR A WORD YOU SAY"

6 November 1946

Stalin, replying to questions asked him by the American press, deprecated talk of tension between Russia and America. He discussed amiably the possibilities of co-operation in German reconstruction, of making peace treaties and of disarmament. But Soviet propaganda against the Western democracies continued with undiminished sharpness.

"HULLO! THE YANKS ARE EXPERIMENTING WITH THEIR BOMB AGAIN . . ."

BLAST ACROSS THE ATLANTIC

7 November 1946

The British received a severe set-back to hopes for revival when the Office of Price Administration in the U S closed down and virtually all American price controls were removed. To the British the sharp rise in prices in the U S meant a rapid shrinkage in the real value of their loan from America; greater difficulty in meeting their obligations to release current sterling from control; a reversal of progress towards balancing their international accounts; and a heavy jolt to their plans for full employment, basic to British policy.

"WHERE'S THE BETTER BRITAIN WE FOUGHT FOR?"
"DOWN THERE"

BURIED TREASURE

31 December 1946

In days of shortage of raw materials and shrunken markets, Britain had one primary commodity of which there was no foreseeable shortage and for which there were hosts of eager customers—coal. After years of inefficiency and decline, the mines had been nationalised, but post-war stringency had delayed, except in a few cases, up-to-date equipment; mining was an unpopular occupation among the youth; and at the beginning of 1947 there was a shortage of highly trained and able personnel not only at bottom but also at top levels.

"YOU'RE A FATHER!"

15 November 1946

When Molotov proposed at the UN, first, the flat unqualified prohibition of the atom bomb; and, second, disclosure by members of the U N of the numbers of their armed forces abroad, he seemed to score propaganda points over the Western Powers. But the British and American delegates suggested improvements. "To make sure no one makes atom bombs, there must of course be international inspection? And why stop at disclosing armed forces abroad? Why not all mobilised forces whether at home or abroad?" ... Molotov hurriedly changed his ground.

LIGHT IN A KREMLIN WINDOW

1 January 1947

As 1947 dawned, Moscow was preparing for the reception
of a new Four-Power Conference of the Foreign Ministers.
Stalin again expressed a benign opinion that there had been
no deterioration of the relations between the Soviet and
American peoples, but only misunderstandings between their
two Governments. For his part he wanted more meetings
of statesmen, expansion of world trade, more exchange of
culture and information and an international police force.
These words were cordially welcomed by optimists in
western countries as a hopeful sign.

CONTROL OF
ATOMIC ENERGY

"AFTER YOU, MY TRUSTY ALLY"

15 January 1947

When Molotov and American spokesmen like Senator
Vandenberg tried to get down to business concerning the
UN and atomic energy, the difficulties appeared to be
about the *how* and the *when* of " inspection and control."
Russia flatly rejected the U S Commission's proposal to set
up an international controlling organ with the functions of
ownership, management, licensing and supervision as a
" violation of sovereignty." The Russians would not be
" inspected and controlled" until the Americans shared
their atomic secrets; and the Americans would not share
their atomic secrets until the Russians were " inspected
and controlled."

TIME'S CHANGES

13 March 1947

A second difficulty was about *how* the "inspection and control" was to be done. Russia flatly rejected the U S Atomic Energy Commission's proposal to set up an international controlling organ with the functions of ownership, management, licensing and supervision. This, objected Gromyko, would violate national sovereignty and would involve undue interference. Political "old hands" commented with surprise that, for the purposes of this debate at least, Soviet Russia had become the champion of nationalism, the U S of internationalism.

RETURN TO DUNKIRK

4 March 1947

Bidault, French Foreign Minister, believed in the need to revive German industry to make her self-supporting, but the French remembered the two world wars and were apprehensive of the risks of a third. As one of a series of treaties among the European countries, to reassure France and secure her co-operation, Bevin signed with Bidault an Anglo-French treaty of alliance at Dunkirk, scene of historic events in the war.

"HIS EXCELLENCY THE SECRETARY OF STATE FOR THE U S A"

16 March 1947

The Communists seemed to be winning the civil war in
Greece when the Foreign Ministers' Conference at Moscow
was shaken by the announcement by President Truman
from Washington of a new policy: The U S, as an
" investment in world freedom," in future would actively
assist free peoples to resist attempts to impose totalitarian
regimes upon them. As a start, the U S would help the
Greek Government to defend itself in its war against the
Communist aided revolutionaries.

IT ALL DEPENDS ON HOW YOU LOOK AT IT

26 March 1947

The Foreign Ministers still disagreed about Germany.
Marshall (U S) and Bevin (Britain) wanted to go slow on
reparations and build up German " peace " industry so
that the Western zones could pay their way. Bidault
(France) thought it would be difficult to separate " war "
industry from " peace " industry, and feared a revival of
Germany's power to make war. Molotov (USSR) wanted
more bulk removals of industrial plant, current output and
foreign assets as reparations.

"WHAT VERY LONG ARMS YOU HAVE, DEAR"

22 April 1947

While the Moscow Conference remained locked in a clinch about German and Austrian treaties, Bevin took the opportunity to press his offer of a year before to extend the Anglo-Russian treaty of alliance to fifty years. The Soviet Government here personified in Vishinsky, were willing, upon condition Britain should not join any hostile bloc. The current Moscow attitude implified that this would mean in effect ditching the U S and joining the Soviet bloc. Bevin drew back embarrassed.

"WHICH HAND WILL YOU HAVE, TOVARICH?"

17 June 1947

U S Secretary of State Marshall outlined a plan to aid
Europe, including Britain, Russia, and "everything west of
Asia." If European countries brought all their national
plans together, America offered financial and material help
to revive a working economy in the world. Moscow pur-
ported to see in this just a repetition of Truman's
declaration of three months before concerning Greece,
whereby the U S offered aid to free peoples resisting
totalitarian pressure. The whole idea was, to Moscow, an
attempt to enslave Europe with dollars.

"NO HURRY, MATE. YOU'RE A HUNDRED YEARS TOO LATE ANYWAY"

25 July 1947

The attempt to settle the troubles of the Netherlands with its East Indies by forming a United States of Indonesia and a Netherlands-Indonesian Union suffered a hitch, when Dutch troops were sent to "help" clean up violence and destruction. The Government of the Indonesian Republic protested that keeping law and order was a job for its police, not for Dutch troops. Bevin and Nehru, about to complete the transfer of power to India, deplored the impatient Dutch approach to the "new spirit of Asia."

"NOSES LEFT!"

9 July 1947

South-eastern European countries within the Soviet sphere turned hopefully towards the Marshall plan. Poland and Hungary began to consider the idea, Czechoslovakia accepted. But Moscow ruled otherwise, after Molotov had visited Paris to hear more. A plan to help the revival of prosperity in Europe flatly opposed any plan for a Communist Europe arising from frustration and failure. Moscow warned U S off and made preparations to bind its Eastern satellites more closely to itself.

SURVEYING THE SITE

15 July 1947

As a first step to the Marshall plan, the European statesmen met in Paris to draw up a balance sheet of needs and resources, to see how they could help one another and how much American aid was required to put Europe on its feet. Bidault, for France, said that the resources of Germany should be used for everybody, including the Germans, which was interpreted as meaning that the restrictions of the Potsdam Agreement would not be regarded as inviolate.

CLAY MODEL

5 August 1947

When the U S (General Clay) and British Military Governors in Germany produced the plan for raising the level of production in the Anglo-American bi-zone, Bidault was worried, Bevin only slightly less so. All the industries restricted in the Potsdam Agreement got higher targets and permitted steel production rose sharply. The French had grave anxiety about the risks that went with the American insistence on encouragement of German private enterprise under a general control unlikely to be permanent once the industry of the Ruhr, the heart of aggressive power, began to revive. The British had wanted public ownership; the French had wished all the governments concerned to have seats on the board of control.

DOLLARS WITH STRINGS

27 August 1947

The rise in prices in U S had taught the British a sharp lesson concerning the reality of their dependence on America. Other nations had felt the pinch also and Britain's creditors demanded to be paid in dollars instead of pounds, to pay for their food imports. There was such a rush on Britain's stock of dollars that the loan from America nearly disappeared altogether. To meet the emergency, the U S and Britain agreed to suspend sterling convertibility. Some American critics had always regarded Britain's trade preferences within the Commonwealth and Empire as obstructive, and took the opportunity to press for their removal.

DID SOMEONE SAY "AN INTERNATIONAL FORCE"?

26 September 1947

As the mandatory Power in Palestine, it was Britain's job
to keep order. The UN Committee decided upon Independence and Partition. But during the transition they
could furnish only authority, no troops. The U S Government suggested that another 100,000 immigrants be admitted
forthwith, but declined to share the responsibility. Britain
asked how it could be expected to carry out these changes
single-handed. Although an international force was suggested it came to nothing. Within Palestine the illegal
armies became bolder, and stepped up a violent campaign
to force the withdrawal of the British, and clear the ground
for a war against the Arabs to establish a Jewish State.

"MY, AIN'T IT GOING TO BE TOUGH FOR THOSE GUYS IF SHE DON'T COLLAPSE"

10 October 1947

Soviet propaganda accounted for American policy as arising from imminent economic and financial crises. The Marshall plan, said Moscow, was an attempt of the U S to save itself by " enslaving Europe with dollars "; or, to put it in less passionate terms, by using its credit possibilities to expand its external markets. Soviet policy appeared to be based upon the firm expectation of an early collapse of American Capitalism.

WHEN DOCTOR'S DISAGREE

19 September 1947

As a change from the Soviet denunciations of the bolstering-up by Britain and America of the Greek Government, Marshall demanded that the U N should consider the great numbers of troops and quantity of material which the Communists were sending to help the Greek guerillas. The U N should discuss this and similar situations, said Marshall, if it wanted to keep healthy. Vishinsky, on the other hand thought the U N should try to lead a quiet life and, in this case, avoid excitement.

58

"LOOK WHAT WE'VE GOT FOR DINNER! PICTURE-POSTCARDS FROM UNCLE JOE!"

COMINFORM MAIL

14 October 1947

While Soviet Russia was preparing to consolidate her position against the Marshall Plan, Communist Parties in Europe proceeded in advance to obstruction and sabotage. Their activities in France and Italy, amounting in the view of Marshall to " barefaced efforts to overthrow the governments " had been rewarded with setbacks for their Party at municipal elections. Duclos and Togliatti, the French and Italian Party leaders, found their followers not much interested in news from Moscow of the establishment of a new organ of unity, the Communist Information Bureau, " Cominform."

TOEING THE NEW LINE

18 November 1947

Moscow explained that the new Cominform was not the old
Comintern, but an information bureau for nine Communist
Parties to " exchange experiences " and to " defend their
independence and sovereignty." Politburo member Zdhanov,
however, with more candour said that it was to head the
resistance to the U S " plan to enslave Europe," and it
was soon evident that in practice it was to be the organ
whereby the Party leaders, " advised " by Moscow, could
formulate precise Party " lines " for the satellite States.
Leaders like those represented in this cartoon, Gottwald of
Czechoslovakia, Thorez of France, Rakosi of Hungary,
and Togliatti of Italy, whose support included non-Party
" Popular Front " elements, foresaw difficulties at home.

FRENCH DEMOCRA

LOW

ROCKING BOAT

26 November 1947

In France a trial of strength followed. Social disorder
arising from financial instability, rising wages, rising prices
and shortage of consumer goods, sabotage and strikes
involving two million railwaymen, miners and civil servants,
brought anarchy in sight. Prime Minister Schuman had
hard work to keep afloat his " Third Force " between the
Communists on the left, led (in the absence of Thorez) by
Duclos, agitating for a general strike, and the " Rally-of-
the-French-People on the right," led by de Gaulle,
advocating constitutional changes and " strong measures."

THE SAINT AND THE TIGER

20 January 1948

The bloody communal clashes which followed the institution
of the new States of India and Pakistan halted when Gandhi
began a fast which he undertook to continue until death if
Hindus and Muslims did not behave more generously to
one another. Leaders of all communal groups promised to
carry out the conditions he laid down for restoring harmony.

TOUCH OF A VANISHED HAND

3 February 1948

Bitter fighting over the disputed accession of Kashmir to India, rioting, burning, looting and bloodshed arising from the communal hatred of Hindus and Moslems came to a climax when Gandhi was assassinated by a member of the extremest right-wing Hindu organisation Mahasabha. Nehru's government arrested its leaders but uproar continued. The loss of the restraining influence of the legendary " Father of India " was grievous.

PATH TO RECOVERY

21 January 1948

Britain was cutting her imports to the bone and trying to
expand her exports, but so were other countries and customers were scarce.   Despite efforts of Cripps, British
Chancellor of Exchequer, to minimise the drain on dollar
and gold reserves, to keep the maximum amount of international trade going, and to nurse the sterling area, American
experts judged that, with Britain putting her best foot
forward, her large dollar deficits were unlikely to be met
for several years—say about 1952.

HERE WE GO——WHOOSH!

13 February 1948

After a period of soaring inflation, U S stock and commodity markets broke and prices went back to where they were when Marshall Aid estimates were first made in the previous October. There was now some anxiety as to whether the price decline might lead the U S into a depression, but this did not eventuate.

"WHO'S NEXT TO BE LIBERATED FROM FREEDOM, COMRADE?"

2 March 1948

Soviet Russia, through its agency the Cominform, hastened
to tighten her hold on her satellite States in preparation for
counter-action and obstruction to the Marshall plan. Shifts
of power in Hungary and Rumania strengthened the power
of their Communist parties and resulted in closer integration
of their economies with that of Soviet Russia. By a coup
the Communists in Czechoslovakia seized full power and
purged opposition parties, politicians and officials suspected
of Western sympathies. This flagrant and ruthless suppres-
sion of political democracy deeply shocked the Western
peoples.

"——AND ALL BUILT FROM THE ROCKS THROWN BY YOU"

19 March 1948

The United States perhaps more than any country was moved by what happened in Czechoslovakia and by anxiety as to what might happen to Greece, Turkey, France and Italy. Washington forgot its desire to limit armaments and decided to build up national defence. Truman said the determination of the free countries of Europe to protect themselves would be matched with an equal determination of the US to help them, and he promised to meet any indirect aggression with " immediate action." A cover-campaign of abuse from Moscow had the effect of solidifying American public opinion.

"I should like it to be clearly understood that this is to be only an illusion"

SAWING THROUGH A WOMAN

13 April 1948

Both Molotov and Marshall advocated German unity, but to Molotov it had to be Communist unity, and to Marshall it had to be anything but Communist unity. Each accused the other of dividing Germany into two " blocs," but Germania could console herself with the promise of both that all would be well when the other found out his mistake.

ITALIAN ELECTION RESULT

22 April 1948

The Italian Communists were bitterly disappointed at securing only 31% of the vote at the Parliamentary elections, and inclined to blame Molotov's violent propaganda and Soviet insistence on the Cominform "line" as main causes of the lost ground for having frightened away "fellow-travellers." The consolidation of anti-Communist Parties in Italy dimmed Togliatti's hopes of a conquest of power.

UN-DEMOCRATIC ACTIVITIES

24 August 1948

Had the calculated aim of Soviet propaganda been to provide the U S to anti-Communist fury, it amply succeeded. Continuous abuse from Moscow press and radio and melodramatic incidents such as the attempt in New York to kidnap two Russian teachers from America combined to carry the watchdog enquiries of the Sub-Committee of Un-American Activities beyond the pale of reason into that of emotion. Sometimes, to the outside world, the efforts of the latter looked like an anti-Red witch hunt.

"WHAT CAN YOU DO TO START THE SERVICE AGAIN?"
"I CAN SELL YOU TICKETS."

FARES, PLEASE

31 August 1948

In Berlin, after the Soviet Military Governor had objected to the currency reform separately introduced in western zones as causing confusion in Berlin, which " lay in and economically formed part of the Soviet zone," the Russians attempted to complete the absorption process by edging the Western Powers out altogether. The Soviet Deputy Governor, on the excuse that the established transport services and corridors needed repairs, announced new traffic regulations amounting to a land and water blockade between the Western zone and Berlin. Molotov hinted that the blockade might be ended if the Western Powers gave way on the currency question.

THE RUN-AROUND

16 September 1948

British, French and U'S envoys went to Moscow to have straight talks about the Berlin currency and the blockade. Molotov and Stalin were very obliging, agreement was reached and a directive was sent to Sokolovsky, the Soviet Military Governor of Berlin. He disregarded it and referred the envoys back to Moscow. The Soviet Government upheld him and disregarded the agreement also, referring the envoys back again to Sokolovsky. It became clear that Moscow was giving the Western Powers the " run-around " and that its intention was to acquire complete control over Berlin. But the Western Powers developed an efficient air-lift of supplies which kept their zones from being starved out and finally broke the blockade.

LOCKOUT

28 September 1948

The Berlin talks went from bad to worse when Soviet sector police put a cordon around the *Stadthaus*, dismissed officials of the City Assembly and refused admittance to British and US Deputy-Commandants. Protests were answered with Soviet accusations that the Western Powers were using the unrest to " hammer together an aggressive military bloc directed against the Soviet Union."

"HEY! NEW SURPRISE MOVEMENT!"

5 October 1948

The debate at the UN on the control of atomic energy was enlivened when Vishinsky unexpectedly announced that Soviet Russia might be willing to relinquish a little of her national sovereignty for the good of humanity and was not opposed to inspection—if the international control body carrying out the inspection were not like that which had been proposed, and if, whatever it might be, its doings were subject to the principle of unanimity, veto and all. The Western Powers heard this without enthusiasm.

"L'EUROPE, C'EST MOI!"

19 November 1948

Planners of European security had a critic in General
de Gaulle, leader of the new formidable French " Rally,"
who thought their plans for reviving Germany as a bulwark
against Soviet Russia were both risky and futile. He condemned a defence system based on Britain. He favoured
splitting it up into three theatres, with France in charge of
Western Europe and North Africa.

THERE ARE OTHER WAYS OF GETTING TO THE WEST THAN GOING WESTWARD

24 November 1948

In China the crumbling of Chiang Kai-shek's Nationalist armies before the rapid advance of the Communist troops opened up speculations as to how far a Communist China might lend itself to the interests of Moscow. Soviet leaders had not expected Mao Tse-tung's success and had given him little help or encouragement. But Mao's Communist Party was modelled upon the example of the Soviet Union and he had said it was " an integral part of the international anti-imperialist campaign."

"OH YEAH?"

7 January 1949

President Truman had just proposed to Congress an extensive
programme of liberal legislation to embody the promise of
equal rights and opportunities proclaimed by the founders
of the American Republic. But little of this got past the
radio obstruction of Soviet Russia or the Cominform States,
where a vicious propaganda campaign continued to describe
Truman as the leader of a warmongering imperialist Wall
Street clique exploiting a gigantic American concentration
camp of slave labour.

77

"CIEL, DO YOU HAVE TO LAY IT ON ME: "

1 December 1948

The idea of an international authority for control of the Ruhr was agreed by the Occupying Powers, the U S, Britain and France. But to McNeil (Britain) and the Americans, Schuman repeated the French protest that so long as this did not involve political separation of the Ruhr area from Germany, and the mines and industries continued to be privately owned by Germans, the menace remained—particularly for France.

THE IRRESISTIBLE MEETS THE IMMOVABLE

15 February 1949

The trial of Cardinal Mindszenty for treason and currency
offences in Hungary brought to a head the antagonism of
the Roman Catholic Church towards the Communist Party.
The Cardinal "confessed," but the Vatican excommunicated
all those concerned with the trial.   On balance, historically,
the Vatican had been happier with totalitarian régimes than
with democracies.   In recent times it had found Mussolini's
Fascist régime in Italy tolerable and had supported
Franco in Spain.   The key to Vatican policy was to be
found in the assertion of the Church's fundamental right
to conduct the religious training of Catholic children.   The
Communist leaders were building up their own religion and
were equally determined to have the children.

TRIUMPH——AND DEFEAT

4 February 1949

An armistice in Palestine was negotiated with the help of a United Nations mediator. The ancient dream of a Jewish Home in Palestine had materialised in the State of Israel, achieved, however, not in peace and goodwill as had been hoped, but through a successful campaign of terrorism and assassination followed by war. Friends who had striven in the past for justice to the Jewish people were now uneasily doubtful whether complete justice had been done to the Arabs.

"THERE, YESTERDAY, WERE WE"

23 March 1949

900,000 Palestinian Arab refugees camped in miserable
conditions over the frontier limit of the new State of Israel,
posed a formidable problem for international relief organisations to cope with. Jews abroad, with memories of the past
of their race, thought that Ben Gurion and Moshe Sharet
of the Israeli Government should take the opportunity
to make a gesture of compassionate sympathy. But Israel
had little money and was already overcrowded by the tidal
wave of new immigrants.

IT WON'T BE LONG NOW

18 March 1949

When Moscow found that Tito would not obey the Cominform " line " in all things, but had ideas of his own for Jugoslavia, it first reasoned with him, then coaxed, then went purple in the face, growling ominous threats. His recalcitrance was a set-back to Soviet hopes in Greece and Italy. Tito, knowing what was coming, protected himself by purging the Jugoslavian Army of Cominform sympathisers, tightening up his frontiers, and vigorously answering back the bitter press and radio campaign coming from his obedient Cominform neighbours, Bulgaria, Hungary and Rumania.

"YOUR PLAY, JOE"

6 April 1949

The U S decided to do for European defence what it
was doing for European economic revival and offered to
help with arms and dollars, if the European States pooled
their defence resources. The U S, Britain, France and nine
other European States signed the North Atlantic Treaty
whereby they undertook to unite their efforts for a common
defence of the North Atlantic area. With the U S as a
senior partner, collective security for non-communist
Europe became more of a possible reality. The world
waited to see how the Moscow strategists would counter-
play.

CARGO OF HYPOCRISY

5 July 1949

The distribution of food throughout Britain was threatened when the unloading of supplies at the ports was stopped by an " unofficial " strike of dock-workers. The strike was ostensibly in sympathy with two crews involved in a dispute between the Communist-dominated Canadian Seamen's Union and the International Seafarers' Union. British Union leaders denounced Communist expressions of sympathy with the workers which shielded manœuvres obviously designed to break up and capture the Unions.

WELCOME

27 July 1949

Western European countries promptly ratified the North Atlantic treaty, and interest then turned to ways and means. France was concerned to secure " the necessary guarantees " about French representation on the organs to be set up and about obtaining from the U S " the arms and equipment indispensible for the French armies."

"SOMETHING'S WRONG. IT SHOULD BE ONLY CAPITALIST STATES THAT
ARE 'INCAPABLE OF HARMONIOUS CO-OPERATION AND THUS CARRY WITHIN
THEMSELVES THE SEED OF THEIR OWN DISRUPTION'."

DOUBT IS BORN

23 August 1949

Tito maintained that he and his Jugoslavia regime were still
Communist, and that his dispute with Moscow and the Cominform concerned only his resistance to Russian domination
and dictation. This put the Moscow dialecticians into
a theoretical false position from which they could only
extricate themselves by finding that Tito was not a Communist after all but a Fascist and an imperialist aggressor.
Thereupon a Soviet propaganda campaign began against
Tito unequalled for viciousness and bitterness since the
heyday of Goebbels and the Nazis in 1939.

BITTER FRUIT

30 August 1949

Although Secretary of State Acheson said that the elections in Western Germany represented a victory for moderation, others were less optimistic. In a French analysis, the 18 million Nazi electors of 1933, half of whom still lived in the Western zone, had provided a part of the 2½ million votes polled by the Nationalist parties. The balance of the former Nazi voters had supported the centre or left-wing parties, some of whose leaders had spoken during the campaign in a singularly nationalistic vein. " This proved that Germany did not yet measure the extent of the crimes perpetrated by Nazism, nor feel proper regret."

INS AND OUTS

25 August 1949

" A sound and expanding world economy was essential to world peace. . . . The United States was trying to expand the exchange of goods and services among nations. It was not engaged in a charitable enterprise. Mutual adjustment, concession and co-operation was not easy," said President Truman re financial talks with Britain and Canada at Washington. It was felt in Britain that there was little chance of establishing equilibrium in world trade until the US modified its tariff to admit more goods from its debtor countries in the outside world.

ANOTHER OF THOSE WINGLESS CHICKENS?

10 August 1949

Urged by the U S, Europe had taken two steps forward in the direction of Western Union. " Benelux," the economic union of Belgium, the Netherlands and Luxembourg; and the Five-Power Brussels Treaty of mutual assistance and economic co-operation. Now a Council of Europe was to be set up and an Assembly was to meet at Strasbourg. At first Britain was cold to the Council, partly because of her existing tie-up with her self-governing Dominions, the interests of which might conceivably conflict with those of a United Europe; and because she feared some possible interference with the full development of British social democratic ideals.

"EFFECTIVE INTERNATIONAL CONTROL OF ATOMIC WEAPONS"

30 September 1949

Vishinsky again condemned delays in the adoption of "practical measures for unconditional prohibition of atomic weapons and for the establishment of adequate strict international control," the nature of which he left vague, except that they would entail a control agency subject to the Security Council where Russia could obstruct proceedings by exercising its veto.

PEOPLE'S CHOICE

18 October 1949

The Western Powers decided to end military government in their zones and established at Bonn a Federal German Republic to give the German people maximum possible self-government consistent with occupation. Moscow protested and hurriedly gave its blessing to a rival Democratic German Republic set up in the Eastern zone, the Government of which proceeded to reverse the acts of the Federal Government. The Western Powers affirmed that while the Federal Government had come about according to the fundamental principles of democracy, the Eastern Government had been created by fiat and had no legal validity.

PARTNERS FOR THE DANCE

4 November 1949

The question of whether the Federal German Republic
should take part not only in plans for economic recovery,
but in the defence of Western Europe depended on an
improvement in Franco-German relations. Hindrances
from the German point of view were France's claim to
the Saar and her attitude concerning the Ruhr industries.
Although Bidault realised that the German problem could
only be solved in the framework of European unity, France
was loth to see Germany have an army again and he had
to be cautious. Anglo-American fear was that if Adenauer
could not show a brighter prospect to his supporters in
Germany, they might turn to other leaders.

MARCH OF SCIENCE

20 January 1950

An atomic explosion had been heard shortly before in the USSR. In the U S the Atomic Energy Commission was directed to continue work on the hydrogen or super-bomb. The world shuddered. Church leaders divided on the moral issue involved, but united in prayer. Common people found little comfort in the assumption that the U S had the ingenuity and resources to keep well ahead of Russia. No progress had taken place towards an agreement on atomic energy.

"SHALL WE RECOGNISE HIM? THE QUESTION IS WILL HE RECOGNISE US?"

3 January 1950

Chinese Communist troops routed Chiang Kai-shek's Nationalist armies and soon had all China under their control. The question of recognising the new Communist Government in Peking arose. The Communists blamed the US for supplying arms and encouragement to the defeated Nationalists. Under the Cairo, Yalta and Potsdam agreements, the important strategic island of Formosa was to be restored to China—but that was Chiang Kai-shek's China and this was Mao Tse-tung's. US Secretary Acheson thought recognition would be premature. But Mao was visiting Stalin in Moscow and it is doubtful whether he cared.

A LITTLE DIFFERENCE IN TIMING

10 January 1950

A difference appeared between Britain and the U S about China. India and Pakistan had promptly recognised the new régime, and after Bevin talked to Pacific and Asian delegates to the Commonwealth Conference at Colombo, Britain followed suit. U S Secretary Acheson, however, delayed decision. In America, angry voices protested against recognition. Overseas, a touchy situation was created on the island of Formosa, now the refuge of Chiang and the remains of his army, which Washington regarded as Chinese territory and as such entitled to receive economic aid.

THE STATE OF THE KING BUSINESS

28 March 1950

The Voice of the People was vexing two European Royalties. In Belgium a general election and a *consultation populaire* were held on the issue of whether King Leopold should return to the Throne or not, but the results were inconclusive. Rightly or wrongly, the King was blamed for his conduct during the world war. Ugly cleavages appeared among the people before Leopold decided to abdicate. In Greece, elections had shown a heavy poll for the Democratic Front and the Greek " strong man," Plastiras. But King George disliked Plastiras. So he side-stepped and skilfully manipulated the advent of another shaky and unpopular, but more manageable, government.

PRIORITY

19 April 1950

Defence expenditure in France had reached 8.2 per cent of the national income. In Britain the new programme had increased it from 8 to 10 per cent. Misgivings were heard about whether rearmament might not undermine the efforts to achieve economic and financial stability which was one of the main elements in the defensive potential. Collective effort was called for, not merely an addition of national endeavours. It could not be made without substantial U S assistance, and, even so, the strain on Western Europe would be great.

PEACE THE MESSENGER

12 April 1950

The Western Powers knew that there could be no holding the Western frontiers if Germany were left a military vacuum, and that sooner or later the question must arise of whether or not Germany should be allowed to have troops to take part in Western defence. But Adenauer now wanted to bargain for concessions before he agreed. The Western Powers shied away from the idea for the time being, especially since a hint of amiability from Russia had started them hoping again, and they felt that re-arming Germany certainly would not contribute to any possible improvement in relations with the Soviet.

"AHEM! I HOPE I DON'T COME AT AN INCONVENIENT MOMENT"

10 May 1950

Trygve Lie, the UN Secretary-General, decided to visit
Stalin personally in Moscow, to try and break the deadlock
between the Great Powers. In his unique capacity as an
official not of one nation but of all, he sought, in particular,
a friendly talk on the general international situation, Chinese
representation in the United Nations, the " cold war " and
the control of atomic energy; in general, to persuade the
Soviet leaders to adopt a more conciliatory attitude. They,
preoccupied with other matters, were polite but vague.

SCHUMAN SYMPHONY

17 May 1950

France thought there were too many political obstacles against Germany's bold suggestion of a Franco-German economic union to end their long-standing disputes. But French Foreign Minister Schuman decided to make a step in that direction by proposing that the two countries pool their production of coal and steel in a supra-national organisation open also to other countries. Belgium, Italy, Luxembourg and the Netherlands agreed to join. The response of Britain was approving but cautious. Bevin wanted to know more about the possible consequences to a socialist country with ties to a Commonwealth.

THE NEXT THING IS TO RAISE THE WALL

24 May 1950

The Commonwealth countries had drawn together for the Colombo Conference in January to elaborate comprehensive plans for the economic development of south-east Asia to avoid the spread of Communism. When they met again in Sydney in May to face the hard problem of how to turn their ideas into realities, find the resources and persuade non-Commonwealth countries in the area to co-operate in the enterprise, the situation had become worse. Guerilla warfare in Malaya in which Communist China was assumed to have a hand had made the situation much worse.

DARK HORSE FOR THE BERLIN DERBY

26 May 1950

It was learned that, despite their pledge to outlaw militarism in Eastern Germany, the Russians were training a German army between 200,000 and 300,000 strong disguised as a People's Police Force, with designs on the city of Berlin. Nervous tension was felt in the West as the time approached for the Whitsun rally of " Free German Youth," which was to take place in the Soviet zone. Malenkov was said to have replaced Zhdanov as the Soviet leader concerned with the affairs of the Cominform satellites.

"NOBODY HERE BUT US KOREANS"

28 June 1950

Without warning, large, well organised and well equipped
forces from North Korea crossed the 38th Parallel into
South Korea. It was evident that the North Koreans had
resources far beyond their internal capabilities. They were
deploying Russian-made tanks and fighter-planes. The
Western democracies saw the hand of Russia behind the
invasion, attempting to destroy an Asiatic experiment in
democracy and to gain a strategic advantage regarding
Japan. The Soviet " line " was equally clear, but in reverse.
The provocative South, they said, had attacked the peaceful
North under the direction of American military advisers.
The U S had " trampled on the UN Charter " by acts of
aggression against both Korea and China.

HISTORY DOESN'T REPEAT ITSELF

30 June 1950

The old League of Nations was said to have given itself the
death blow by failing to take a strong hand against Italy's
invasion of Abyssinia in 1935. Its successor, the United
Nations, was not repeating that error when fifteen years
later its survival was threatened by an equally blatant
flouting of its authority. South Korea was a state established by the UN with a government elected under its
supervision. The Security Council ordered the invaders to
cease-fire and withdraw. US naval and air forces had
already moved to help the South, when the Council called
on Member States to check what Truman called " this effort
to see whether under existing world conditions, armed
aggression paid."

PHONEY PEACE PARADE

4 July 1950

North Korean invaders appeared to be overwhelming the defenders of the South by sheer weight of numbers. Britain asked Russia to use its influence to effect a peaceful settlement. Moscow promptly mounted a propaganda campaign for " peace." According to the USSR the UN intervention was an American enterprise solely, and the way to stop the war was to stop the Americans. The Soviet Government said that it maintained the principle of non-interference, and it held that the Koreans had a perfect right to settle their own affairs in their own way. All would have been well if the South had accepted the recent proposals of the North for unity along Communist lines.

"US—THAT SPELLS 'US'"

25 July 1950

The Soviet Government held that the UN action was
invalid because the Soviet representatives had absented
themselves, which counted as a veto, and the Chinese
Communists were not represented at all. Fifty-three member-
States of the UN approved the armed intervention. The
Commonwealth showed a striking unity of view, and Britain,
Australia and New Zealand promptly offered naval and
land forces. France, which was already fighting a tough
war against Communist armies in Indo-China, promised
active assistance in the interests of collective security.

RETURN OF THE PRODIGAL

1 August 1950

Before Malik, Soviet delegate to the UN who had walked out of the Security Council some weeks before when South Korea was about to be discussed, took his seat as President for the new session of the Council, it was heralded that he was going to place on the agenda new peace proposals for a settlement in Korea. These turned out to be: (a) that a representative of the Peking Communist Government be recognised as the lawful representative of China on the Council; and (b) that the United States " aggression " against Korea be stopped.

"HOLD IT!"

9 August 1950

General MacArthur, whose views notoriously disagreed with those of his superiors at Washington, caused anxiety when he visited Chiang Kai-shek at Formosa, where the Nationalist leader lay with the remains of his armies. The General said they had discussed " co-operation for the defence of Formosa." Questions arose about how far this co-operation went. Nehru, Lie and Bevin warned Acheson that Britain, India and the other States concerned were acting according to the UN resolution and had no wish to be committed to the unpredictable adventure of a war with China, especially when, as they thought, it might be just what the Soviet strategists wanted.

EMPTY BOOTS

11 August 1950

After totting up the effective European military forces for the common defence of the North Atlantic area, it was evident that they were not nearly enough, even with generous American assistance. According to some critics, the West at this time was less able to defend itself than had been South Korea. The vulnerable area of Western Germany remained a big problem. The choice of risks between re-arming Germany and undertaking the great additional strains of defending it themselves still vexed the U.S, Britain and France.

THE JUDGE

3 October 1950

Although India had accepted the U N Resolution to intervene in Korea, when the fortunes of war turned and U N forces drove the Northern invaders back over the dividing 38th Parallel, Nehru thought the fighting should stop and negotiations begin. What the United Nations did next, he said, would be watched by the Eastern peoples and in the long run would decide the future of Western influence in Asia.

HERE COMES OLD SPANNER-TOSSER TO "HELP" US

17 October 1950

Weaknesses of UN machinery were revealed by the failure to settle post-war problems or to establish a collective security system. US Secretary Acheson suggested, as possible improvements, a means to circumvent the veto, which prevented the Security Council from dealing rapidly with a crisis; and a plan to build up a force suitable for the service of the UN from special units trained in the national armies of member-states. Vishinsky agreed—except that he objected to any interference with the veto, and to the raising of special troops.

PEACE, IMPERFECT PEACE

1 November 1950

A Peace Congress sponsored by a World Peace Committee at Prague, was to be held at Sheffield. Its aim was to win popular support for Soviet peace proposals. Since these were the familiar oft-rejected wheezes to catch the unwary—aboliton-of-atomic-weapons separated altogether from control-and-inspection; and proportional reduction of armaments only, leaving the Soviet's relative superiority unimpaired and the non-Communist West's inferiority confirmed—the British Government concluded that the Congress was another manœuvre to weaken the resolution of the West to protect itself. Certain delegates were refused entry and the Congress moved back to Prague.

"SOME FEATHERS FOR IT TO FLY WITH, MISTER VISHINSKY"

7 November 1950

Soviet and Cominform Foreign Ministers conferred about
Germany at Prague, and produced a set of proposals for
the Western Powers: a 5-Power pact to work the Potsdam
Treaty, to make a peace treaty with Germany, to prevent
the restoration of its war potential, to withdraw foreign
troops and to remove all restrictions to its becoming a
united democratic and peace-loving State. Bevin, Acheson
and Schuman told Vishinsky that this was a bit late. They
had been trying to realise just these aims for years and all
along had been frustrated by Soviet obstruction. They
had become weary of double-talk and suggested existing
opportunities for co-operation and peace through deeds.

A COMPLICATED QUESTION OF "FACE" FOR THE UN

15 November 1950

The prophets had been proved right and the Chinese had
entered the war, giving out, however, that the twenty-six
divisions they deployed in North Korea were not " official "
but just " volunteers." The UN invited a delegation from
Peking to Lake Success to attempt a solution by mediation
and also to examine the knotty question of Formosa. The
Western Powers knew that the Peking Government could
not afford to " lose face " on these two matters. But they
decided the risk was worth the chance of finding a
peaceful way out.

ALL QUIET ON THE WESTERN FRONT

1 December 1950

With the intervention of Chinese armies the scale of the war in Korea had grown bigger, and reverses suffered by the UN forces began to stretch resources and man-power. Worried critics wondered if they were drifting into " the wrong war." An aggression which threatened the whole fabric of the UN and the hopes of peace and justice it stood for had to be put down. But the establishment of the projected integrated defence forces in Europe was urgent. What might happen now if Russia chose to engineer a crisis against, say, Jugoslavia or Western Germany?

THE THIRD MAN

5 December 1950

Attlee travelled to Washington to talk to Truman. On the points of refusal to appease but readiness to negotiate peace on the basis of UN principles, British and U S foreign policies were identical. There was agreement to disagree over the recognition of the Chinese Communist Government. But the British had two anxieties: lest the U S might involve itself and Britain in full-scale war with China through some reckless action in Formosa; or lest the atom bomb might be used in Korea without their being consulted. . . . Naturally Moscow expressed suspicious curiosity as to what transpired.

"WAIT A BIT, DEAR, WE'RE BUSY WINNING THE WAR"

12 December 1950

The assurance of the Peking delegation to the UN that China
desired a peaceful settlement encouraged thirteen Asian
and Arab countries to make a joint appeal to the Chinese
Government and the North Korean Authorities to declare
that their forces would not cross south of the 38th Parallel
and that they would help to arrange a cease-fire. But the
war was going better for the Communists. Russia said the
appeal was a dodge to gain time for the Americans to
re-group their armies. It got nowhere.

ARMY MEDICAL

13 December 1950

The disagreement about arming Germans for Western defence was patched up by the creation of a defence organisation not on a national but on a European basis, in which German units could be included at the disposal not of German Generals but of a Supreme Commander. German representatives, who were present only as associates, not as members at the Council of Europe which made this decision, raised various objections but in the end Adenauer and a majority agreed.

"IT'S JUST SOME PEOPLE MOVING IN NEXT DOOR"

3 January 1951

If Stalin, Malenkov and Vishinski imagined that the accept-
ance by the Western Powers of a Russian invitation to
hold a conference on German problems would halt NATO
plans, they were mistaken. Arrangements went ahead for
the establishment in Europe of an integrated defence force
of contingents from the participating countries. General
Eisenhower had been appointed Supreme Commander with
an international staff, and was to move into his headquarters
almost at once.

AIN'T LIFE TERRIBLE?

12 January 1951

The wild speeches of some American public men suggesting the settlement of disputes with Russia by dropping bombs on Moscow and with China by opening a full war in partnership with Chiang Kai-shek, gave moderate British opinion intermittent shocks. On the other hand, when the British looked towards Soviet Russia, they feared that without the support of U S the outlook would be black.

"OH WELL, I WAS HAVING INSOMNIA ANYWAY"

16 January 1951

Attlee and Chancellor Gaitskell announced that the cost of Britain's part of the defence programme would rise to £5,000 millions over three years. A rise in production and a fall in consumption were needed. Measures would be necessary to check civilian demand and the standard of living would fall. The Government would try to preserve the social services. British public opinion was already prepared for the bad news.

QUIET VOICE

17 January 1951

As an Asian himself Nehru inclined to disagree with the Western democracies about Asian matters and to regard much of what they indiscriminately called "Communism" as Asian nationalism. He had been a follower of Gandhi in the long struggle for Indian freedom, and he was not deaf to Mao Tse-tung's contention that the affairs of Asia should be run by the people of Asia themselves, not by the Americans. He thought that specially interested countries like Russia and China should be given a fair chance to co-operate in making a peace treaty with Japan; and that something should be done about handing Formosa back to China, whatever government it had. Above all, he flatly opposed all talk of open war on China as not only wrong but likely to prove disastrous.

INSCRUTABLE MAO

30 January 1951

The delegation from the Chinese Communist Government which visited the UN proved to be tough. Mao Tse-tung's terms were the withdrawal of all foreign troops from Korea and Formosa and the acknowledgement of his Government's right to China's place in the UN. With the encouragement of the U S the UN declared China to be the aggressor in Korea. A difference of opinion arose between Austin and Jebb, U S and British delegates respectively, the latter holding that this might end all hopes of reaching a reasonable settlement.

THE BROOD INEVITABLE TO THE NEST

6 February 1951

Moscow protested to the U S, Britain and France against
the North Atlantic Pact and the re-militarism of Germany,
alleging an offensive purpose against Soviet Russia. The
Western Powers' reply was that their military plans were
solely for defence. They reviewed Soviet anti-Western
actions since the end of the war, including the Soviet-
directed seizure of power by Communist minorities in East
European countries, Soviet support of Greek, Malayan and
Indo-Chinese rebels, Cominform propaganda against the
West and the abuse of the veto. It was this chain of events
and the Soviet military preparations which were responsible
for their present policy.

FACING THE FACTS

13 February 1951

The British Government, like other North Atlantic Treaty countries, had accepted the principle of full rearmament, including a measure of military revival for Germany. A body of British opinion feared the risks, social and political, national and international, of equipping the world with modern weapons; but the risks of military weakness in a power-political situation were seen to outweigh them.

TANGLED RELATIONS IN THE MIDDLE EAST

24 July 1951

The war over Palestine had upset the nineteenth-century basis and weakened the European position throughout the Middle East. The Jews blamed the British for helping the Arabs, and the Arabs blamed them for helping the Jews. Defeat had united the Arabs in their League and inflamed militant nationalists particularly in Egypt. To the Western Powers Egypt was the key to the Middle East, but now the Egyptians wished to be free to make their own bargains, about defence, regardless of Western ideas. As a further embarrassment to Britain and its Foreign Secretary Morrison they claimed the Sudan as part of Egypt. On the other hand, Israel was engaged in angry disputes with Iraq and Jordan, Britain's most consistent Arab friend.

"CLEAR OUT, YOU LOT! THE COMPOUND IS ROUND THE CORNER"

1 March 1951

In South Africa, Dr. Malan's new racial policy of separating the voting and representation of coloured and white voters set a fundamental poser for the Commonwealth and Empire. Malan held that the admission of new self-governing Asiatic States like India and Pakistan and the prospective evolution of African colonies into self-governing dominions would destroy the "white" basis of Commonwealth solidarity. He was particularly incensed at the British Government for discussing a future raising of the status of Bechuanaland, Basutoland and Swaziland, territories which Malan had aimed at adding to South Africa. The British reply was that the policy of working towards self-government for colonies within the Commonwealth was traditional and the highest purpose of Empire.

HERE WE GO ROUND THE AGENDA

13 April 1951

Deputies of the British, French, U S and Soviet Foreign Ministers met to see if they could arrange the 4-Power conference on German unity suggested earlier by Russia. This " preliminary " dragged on for weeks, the deputies unable to agree even upon a draft agenda of matters to be discussed. First, Soviet deputy Gromyko wanted a form of wording which would commit the Ministers in advance to a reduction of the armaments of the four Powers, irrespective of the existing size of their armies. The other delegates complained that the conference was to have been about Germany. Then Gromyko wished to have the North Atlantic Treaty debated. The other delegates gave up and went home.

ATMOSPHERICS IN KOREA

28 April 1951

General MacArthur was held by some to have established almost an absolute command over Far Eastern forces. Occasionally he made pronouncements, apparently on his own responsibility, that embarrassed the political strategists in Washington. When he talked publicly of what the " expansion of UN military operations through Chinese coastal bases and interior bases " would mean to China, Washington and London became perturbed at what he might take into his head to do next. President Truman decided to recall MacArthur, and a political storm broke. It was an anxious time to be preparing to resist a new offensive from North Korea.

"WHY NOT? I ONLY RISK ANOTHER BROKEN LEG"

26 June 1951

Malik, Soviet delegate to the UN, broadcasting over a UN network, proposed as a first step towards a Korean settlement that " the belligerents should negotiate for a cease-fire providing for the mutual withdrawal of forces from the 38th Parallel." Despite the continued failures to date of other leads, the Western nations lost no time in following up the hint with discussions as to how the armistice could be negotiated.

CAUSE AND EFFECT

10 July 1951

It was thought in some optimistic quarters that what appeared to be a new desire for peace in Communist quarters justified a relaxing of Western rearmament plans. But others in the contrary, held that if a better spirit of accommodation indeed existed, its inspiration would be the strength of the Western democracies, not their weakness.

THE WAR OF WITS

7 August 1951

A much-heralded " World Youth Festival " in the Soviet
sector of East Berlin was attended by some 11,000 young
people, German and foreign, ranging from 15 to 50. Pro-
cessions with slogans and athletics performed in the Stadium
aroused much enthusiasm on the Communist side of the
fence.

IF ONLY I COULD FEEL SECURE

10 August 1951

Shvernik, Chairman of the Presidium of the Supreme Soviet, wrote to Truman suggesting that the five big powers should sign a treaty to end the cold war. The Western democracies suspected just another manœuvre, probably to force the recognition of the Chinese Communist Government and to upset the signing of the Japanese Peace Treaty, with all the Soviet propaganda turned on to distort the facts to the advantage of the Soviet. So the Foreign Ministers replied that they already had a solemn peace pact to which they had all subscribed in the U N Charter. Why not use that?

MEETING OF THE NEW BOARD

12 July 1951

The Persian Majlis declared its intention to repudiate existing contracts, take over the Anglo-Iranian Oil Company's installations virtually on its own terms and nationalise the Persian oil industry. A new Premier, Dr. Mussadeq, came in, whose lively flow of abusive attack belied his public professions of being a swooning invalid. The British Government requested arbitration on the legality of the take-over, and the Anglo-Iranian Oil Company withdrew its staff, reserving its rights. The new Persian staff, politically keen but technically incompetent, sat down to operate the industry. The big refinery at Abadan slowed down to stop.

IRAN
POLITICAL HOSPITAL

PATIENT: Dr Mossadeq
CONDITION: High fever
weak judgment.

PERSIAN NATIONAL ECONOMY

MOVE OVER, MUSSA! HERE'S ANOTHER ONE SICK

13 September 1951

Britain withdrew the special financial and economic facilities
accorded by it to Iran as a favoured co-operating associate.
Mussadeq, an extremely lively invalid, denounced this as
unfair pressure, and retaliated by inviting the U S (unsuc-
cessfully) to serve an ultimatum to the British Government
calling on it to reopen negotiations on the basis of the
Persian conditions within two weeks or suffer the ejection
of remaining oil staff at Abadan. Meanwhile, with Iran's
income cut and its future sales of oil doubtful, Mussadeq
ordered storage tanks to be filled slowly so that Persian
workers might be occupied as long as possible.

UNEXPECTED MESSENGER OF PEACE

16 August 1951

The Russians had wanted the peace treaty with Japan to be drafted by the Big Four nations alone, with Russia able to block progress by using the veto. When the U S and British Governments circulated a draft with an invitation to attend a Peace Conference to all the nations that had been at war with Japan, Russia found plenty to object to about it. But Gromyko unexpectedly attended the Conference, to the embarrassment of the Western statesmen, who feared he might throw a spanner into the works. But he was satisfied to state the Soviet point of view and refuse to sign.

STOOGE SUITOR

27 September 1951

Soviet efforts having failed to talk the Western Powers out of Federal German participation in not only the economy but the defence of the European community, Eastern Germany now came forward with counter-offers direct to Adenauer. Premier Grotewohl proposed free secret elections for an " all-German Parliament " admitting all democratic parties, and a " guarantee of personal freedom in all parts of Germany." Adenauer took this with a pinch of salt, knowing that Grotewohl was only the stooge for the decisions of Moscow, which were designed to checkmate Washington. He replied that he would be glad to discuss German unity after the inclusion of Federal Germany in the Western defence system.

HOT SEAT

30 October 1951

Difficulties crowded on Britain when the new Churchill Government took office, committed to restoring private enterprise, reducing the cost of living, increasing British prestige abroad and ending austerity. The cost of carrying out the defence programme threatened to throw the national economy out of balance. The withdrawal of British staff from Abadan had damaged British prestige in the Middle East, and Egypt was taking a high-handed attitude about the Sudan and the new proposals for Middle East defence.

MUTUAL WARNING

27 November 1951

The Arab League signed a security pact and talked of forming an Eastern bloc, including besides League members, Persia, Pakistan and Afghanistan, with the eventual addition of the North African States. Anglo-American plans for the defence of the Middle East languished while their " friends " began to dilate on their unsatisfied national aspirations and seemed ready for the risky game of playing off one Cold-War group against the other.

HEAT WAVE FRIVOLITY

28 July 1951

An American proposal to negotiate for bases in Spain was coldly received in Europe. Britain advised against, on the ground that any military or other advantage would be outweighed by the bad effect on Western morale of associating Fascist Spain with the defence of the Western democracies.

IKE'S SQUARE-DANCE CLASS

29. November 1951

Eisenhower's efforts to persuade the West European states to join in one European army were subject to delay and frustration. The small states were accommodating, but Britain, while anxious not to be out of it, still would not be in it. In France, de Gaulle and his powerful " Rally " flatly opposed the idea on the grounds that it would mean the resurrection of the German Army without the least guarantee of its use. Adenauer had to think of the hostile criticism of his Opposition in Germany.

NEXT MOVES TO PEACE

11 January 1952

The Vishinsky method was amply demonstrated at the U N during debate on a resolution recommending means to enable U N members to take part in collective action. First, he did his best to set the states in the Atlantic alliance by the ears against one another by " proving " that U N action in Korea was a private war of aggression by U S and her " satellites "; then he suggested an immediate special meeting of the Security Council to consider how " existing international tensions could be eased, and measures taken to successfully conclude a cease-fire in Korea."

TIME FOR ANTHONY TO VISIT CLEOPATRA

29 January 1952

In Egypt the Government attempted to distract attention
from a revolutionary internal situation by encouraging
nationalist movements to expel the British without further
negotiations for a new treaty about Middle East defence.
An armed clash in the Canal Zone was followed by mob
rioting and burning in Cairo. As King Farouk dismissed
Prime Minister Nahas and began political manœuvres to
save the position, British Foreign Minister Eden stood by
ready, when circumstances permitted, to continue talks on
revision of the 1936 treaty.

143

IT SEEMS THEY NEED A KEYSTONE

19 February 1952

Much of the delay and indecision about the creation of the European defence force was due to uncertainty as to the specific part to be played by Britain. But Eden would go no further than to reaffirm " abiding interest " in the European Defence Community, and the decision of the British Government to maintain armed forces in Europe to contribute to joint defence in association with it. But the means whereby this could be done would have to be considered and discussed, etc., etc.

REVIEWING THE PAPER TROOPS

28 February 1952

The Council of the European Defence Community stated that member nations would provide in 1952—certainly in 1953—" approximately fifty divisions in appropriate conditions of combat-worthiness and 4,000 operational aircraft in Europe—including the United Kingdom—as well as " strong naval forces." Signs were already apparent, however, that some member countries were making heavy weather in attempting to meet the totals of military expenditure fixed for them under a NATO agreement at Lisbon. It was evident that the forecast was highly optimistic.

"OO, GOODY! HERE'S SOMETHING WE CAN CUT!"

22 February 1952

Meeting the heavy costs of the armaments programme in Britain's serious financial position involved drastic economies. Among drastic cuts imposed were those on radio and propaganda services abroad. Critics complained that the presentation of the British case to the world was already poor, that the Communists had had all the best of it in the war of wits, and that the British failed to appreciate that in wars of ideologies, ideas were deadlier weapons than arms.

MAKE THE HOLE A BIT BIGGER

4 March 1952

A serious economic situation had again arisen in France.
The Assembly had approved the total of military expenditure, but refused to pass the new taxes to pay for it. The
Government resigned and the usual depressed procession
of possible successors to the Premiership filed through the
President's chamber seeking some way of overcoming the
unwillingness of the French to pay taxes, and the traditional
preference of the peasant to put his savings into a sock and
bury it.

MIDDLE EAST OLYMPICS

24 July 1952

In Egypt, nepotism, bribery and corruption connected with the supply of inferior material to the army during the Palestine war brought discontent to a head. King Farouk had shuffled governments and promised to clean up the administration too often. He could not avert a bloodless *coup d'etat* by a group of army officers led by General Neguib Mohammed. . . . In Iran, the politically inexperienced Shah was no match for the erratic demagoguery of Mussadeq, who now blamed the catastrophic effect of his policy on the Shah, whom he accused of friendliness towards the British.

EGYPTIAN RUSH-HOUR

7 August 1952

The change-over in Egypt took place without violence. Farouk abdicated and left the country. Neguib proceeded to purge the Egyptian domestic political scene by sacking or arresting politicians and administrators associated with the old régime. To avoid possible unpleasantness there was a general rush to approve and be approved by the new leaders. Churchlll and Eden joined in the applause but wondered what views Neguib had on defence.

Preparations for a
"Peace Conference" are under way
in Peking. It is reported that the
Korean Armistice talks are to be brought
there to show how keen the Chinese are for Peace.

EXHIBIT A

10 September 1952

The truce talks begun in Korea after Malik's radio initiative in July 1951 had been stalled for months. The main question at issue concerned the exchange of prisoners. The North Koreans and Chinese "people's volunteers" rejected all the proposals of the UN representatives including those sponsored by India, particularly the principle of no enforced repatriation. The UN complained bitterly that the Communists had needed a slackening of the war when they were in bad shape, but now they had got through the winter they were prepared to wait out the war, truce or no truce. . . . A news message from China said that it was proposed to hold a Peace Congress in Peking.

"THERE, DEAR. NOBODY
WANTS TO LEAVE YOU OUT"

BEHIND THE DOOR

8 August 1952

Ever since it became uncertain during World War II whether
the British Fleet could always be available to defend the
Pacific Dominions of the Commonwealth, they had looked
to the U S for naval protection. A Pacific Security
Pact between Australia, New Zealand and the U S
(ANZUS) set up a 3-Power Pacific Council in 1951,
and now held its first conference to discuss closer and
regular co-operation to preserve peace in the Pacific area.
This was watched with some mortification in Britain, and
it was asked why the British had not been invited to join.
The Council replied that this would be " premature " but
it would " keep in touch."

MOSCOW "NEW LOOK"

7 October 1952

When Malenkov, instead of Stalin, made the Report to the Communist Party, observers discerned not only the line of succession to Soviet leadership, but also signs of a major switch in Russian tactics. The policy of trying to divide the free nations continued, but in a less openly aggressive manner. The softening was accounted for by the apprehensions of Moscow concerning the foreshadowed joining by Western Germany to the Atlantic Pact and the European Defence Community. The Soviet's argument with the Western Powers proceeded about the nature of the " free " elections which had to precede a unified German Government. In the Soviet's satellite states governments were shuffled and some Communist leaders who had been closely connected with the previous more aggressive policies were discovered to be criminals and purged. But there were no signs of slackening in the increase of Soviet military strength or in the anti-American propaganda.

NEW WEAPON FOR THE FAR EAST

3 February 1953

Newly-elected Eisenhower stated a change in U S policy. The U S fleet which had been used both to ensure that Formosa, Chiang Kai-Shek's headquarters, should not be used as a base for attacks on the Chinese mainland and to prevent attacks from the mainland on Formosa, would no longer be employed to " shield China." Speculation was rife as to whether or not this was a first step towards using Chiang's forces against China, either in a diversionary movement or in the Korea fighting. Those members of the UN who objected to widening the Korean war were accordingly disturbed.

PARADE OF THE HOME GUARD

4 February 1953

Dulles, Secretary of State, and Stassen, head of the Mutual Security Agency in the new administration of President Eisenhower, began their terms of office with a tour of European capitals to see how the plan for a European army was getting along. What they found did not please them. In both France and Germany ratification of the German and the E.D.C. treaties was meeting obstacles. Britain had signed a treaty of mutual assistance with E.D.C. but did not feel able actually to join it because of her overriding association with the Commonwealth. " If there appeared to be no chance of getting unity, the U S might have to do a little ' re-thinking,' " said Dulles ominously.

"WE BROUGHT YOU OUT TO ENJOY YOURSELF, AND ENJOY YOURSELF YOU SHALL!"

UNWILLING AFRICAN

13 February 1953

Many months of examination under two British Governments preceded the decision to form the two Rhodesias and Nyasaland into a Central African Federation. The move was aimed mainly at administrative efficiency and economic improvement, partly at demonstrating an alternative to retrograde racial tendencies in South Africa. But African tribal chiefs in the North had come to fear that Federation meant only the loss of their own local rights to the dominating whites. No Africans attended the final conference which decided to go ahead with the plan. African opposition grew and centred upon the Kikuyu tribe from whom the Mau-Mau recruited bands to raid, burn and kill outlying settlers and their African sympathisers. But British Colonial Secretary Lyttleton, supported by South Rhodesia's Premier Huggins, refused to delay.

155

"SO GLAD YOU CAME——WHEN CAN YOU GO?"

17 February 1953

Britain and Egypt reached agreement on most points about the Sudan, but the situation was complicated by Neguib's representatives having made at the same time differing agreements with various Sudanese political parties. Neguib and his friends amiably assured British Foreign Secretary Eden that they intended to reach a settlement of the Canal Zone question by negotiation, but from their public speeches they seemed to take it as settled that the parley would be merely formal and that Britain would evacuate the Zone forthwith without conditions.

STALIN

EMPTY SHOES

6 March 1953

When Stalin died the world waited to see who would fill his place. For years the personality of the dead leader had been so magnified by all the arts of propaganda that his lieutenants were by comparison insignificant and their characters and capabilities unknown. It was generally expected that the reversion would lie between Malenkov, latterly Stalin's favourite, and the astute veteran Beria; but the interesting question was whether the change of leader would bring a change of policy.

"AH, HIS EXCELLENCY SMOKES ONLY HIS OWN SPECIAL BRAND"

17 March 1953

Marshall Tito visited Britain to discuss a common interest
in resistance to aggression. Although Tito was anxious to
receive full support from the Western Powers if attacked,
he would not undertake to join automatically in any defence
plans of the NATO group. It was realised, however, that
as things stood, if it came to a European war circumstances
would give him no choice as to his allies. Meanwhile
Yugoslavia would establish closer relations with Greece
and Turkey.

VOICE OF SPRING

31 March 1953

The international temperature fell appreciably after the first acts and pronouncements of Moscow under the new Premiership of Malenkov. Within the USSR a scandalous prosecution of Jewish doctors was reversed and an amnesty declared for short-term prisoners. To the outside world official communications were in less denunciatory terms, expressing devotion to peace, and accompanied by various gestures of courtesy. Western governments pondered whether the change of leadership in both the US and the USSR might not make the time propitious for a new attempt to end the cold war. Secretary Dulles, however, accepted the peace talk with reserve and wanted practical evidence of Soviet sincerity.